2019
For Dan
and Jany.
My
Best
Love

My Soul's

Journey

Susan Berard-Goldberg

ISBN 978-1-64559-459-8 (Paperback)
ISBN 978-1-64559-460-4 (Digital)

Covenant Books, Inc.
11661 Hwy 707
Murrells Inlet, SC 29576
www.covenantbooks.com

Dedication

This book is dedicated to Maddie, a fur angel who intervened in my soul's journey and set it on a remarkable course.

Acknowledgments

For my father, who gave me my love of language, and my mother, who gave me my love of books.

For my sister, for her lifelong loyalty and love to our family.

For my husband, for his support and encouragement of my endeavors.

For my three daughters, who have taught me more than I could ever teach them.

For Dr. Susan Berger, EdD, LICSW, for starting me on the road to recollection and recovery.

For Father Francis Signorelli, s.x., and the Xaverian Missionaries of the Fatima Shrine in Massachusetts, the seat of my religiosity.

I have a house inside of me—
A house that people never see;
It has a door through which none pass,
And windows, but they're not of glass.
"Where do you live?" ask folks I meet,
And then I say, "On such a street";
But still I know what's really me
Lives in a house folks never see.
—Rev. S.W. Graffin, *Bob
White's Scrap Book*

In the Beginning: Home

Now the day is done and I
Turn to hear a welcoming cry.
Love is dancing at the door,
I am safe at home once more.
——Author unknown

My childhood house is going to be sold. Wait…I mean my childhood "home." "House" sounds cold. It implies a structure—a place to eat and sleep and have shelter from the elements. A "home" is far different. It is a womb, a cocoon, a bunting of sorts. Hopefully it is the place where one experiences protection and growth, where nurturing and love can lead to everlasting, wonderful memories.

I grew up in a "home" alongside a wonderful mother and father and a much younger sister. We were bonded to one another even though I didn't fully realize it at the time. I know now. I know because whenever one member left, a hole remained in the others.

My parents were the offspring of immigrants who had taught them great values, including a tireless work ethic. They sacrificed throughout their lives to give the best life they could to us—their daughters. We, in turn, learned this devotion well. In later years, my sister and I cared for our parents the way they had cared for us.

Devotion and hard work were not the only things learned in that home. Home was where I learned about respect and how to treat others. It was where I learned about responsibility (and boy, did I learn about that!) and about God. Never in all those years growing up did I entertain the thought that my childhood home would be sold or that my parents wouldn't be there. But life has its plan. Parents become older. They can become ill and die. By the same token, offspring grow up and begin their own lives. So why does it hurt so much? Because home is where my story begins.

The Family

Inside the home is the family. The family consists of the individuals who weave the web and work the magic. A musical of sorts is created with each member playing a very specific part, and each part impacts the other parts. Those in charge must be clear and concise, exercising their power and demands so that the musical will be beautifully and meaningfully executed. The ultimate goal is that this musical will evolve, will improve over time, and be reproduced in the future. The heads of the family are the writers, producers, and directors. The children will obey, learn, and give their best performance. Hopefully, society will benefit as the performers dance on the world's stage.

The Parents: My Mom

Mothers are remarkable. My mom was remarkable. She was selfless and kindhearted, and she had been a tireless worker all her life. As the eldest child in a large immigrant family, she was a "little mother" to many siblings. At the completion of eighth grade, she was forced to quit school and go to work to help support the family. She walked miles to her job in every kind of weather. Every paycheck had to be handed over to her parents. Life was hard. It was for many in those days before and after the Depression. Working hard was part of her being. And she continued to do that for us.

When I was told my mom wouldn't be getting better, that the end was approaching, I couldn't believe it. I refused to believe it! Not my mother. She was tough as nails. She passed and she took a part of me with her. I had lost my first teacher, my best friend, and my confidante. As I now approach the final third of my life, I identify so much more with my mom in her later years—her wit, her wisdom, her fortitude. Two such visits with my mom particularly stand out in my mind. These visits portray much of her personality and maternal instincts.

It was a typical Sunday afternoon. I say typical because, for our family, it was. Each and every Sunday until my parents died was family dinner. I would arrive with my children for Sunday dinner, which would conclude with coffee and long-in-to-the-afternoon conversations. It was a rite of passage, so to speak, handed down from their generation to mine, and my sister's. My daughters loved these dinners. Every special occasion—including birthdays for beloved stuffed animals—was celebrated here. Family birthdays, homecomings from college and camp, school awards, report cards, etc., were noted at these Sunday dinners. If for some reason a dinner was missed, the week just seemed to get off to a bad start. And so, we honored the matriarch and patriarch of our family at these much-anticipated Sunday dinners.

One visit with her, not very long before she left our family home for a nearby nursing facility, stands out in my mind. Her words ring true to me from that day.

It was one of those typical Sunday afternoons. I had gone to my parents for Sunday dinner as I usually did. After coffee and lengthy conversation, I did the dishes. When I finished, my mom was waiting for me in the living room. She was there standing at the bottom of the stairs, holding on to her walker. Mom had suffered a moderate stroke months before. She had recouped remarkably well; all that remained was an imbalance that affected her ability to walk. The walker enabled her to be more ambulatory.

"I need to go upstairs to the attic," Mom said.

I chuckled. "Are you kidding?" I asked with an incredulous voice. But one look at that face and I could tell that there was no kidding involved. I had seen that look so many times over the years—more than I cared to recall. And so, our journey began. The long stairway loomed ahead, high and steep. It could easily have been Mount Everest.

The walker stared at us from the bottom of the stairs as we gingerly made our way up. Step by narrow step, I held up the rear—literally—with my arms braced against her back. Finally, we were at the top. My palms were sweaty, and my heart was racing but not Mom's. Her hands were as dry as a bone. She was ecstatic to have made it to the top. To the right of the landing was a door that opened to the attic.

"I want to go in there," she said.

I opened the door. The attic is very large by most standards. Christmas decorations, large picture frames, and dance recital costumes hung from nails driven into roughhewn beams. An old baby's highchair stood nearby with a forlorn-looking teddy bear sitting in it and waiting anxiously for dinner. A few feet from the open door rested the receptacle of our family's most meaningful treasures—the cedar chest.

"Bring me a chair," Mom ordered. I spotted an old armless oak chair and carried it to my mother's side. She slowly lowered herself onto the seat next to the cedar chest. We both stared at the sleek, though somewhat dusty, mahogany top. The gravity of what was about to happen next hit me. Then…

"Open it. I want to look inside," she said.

I gingerly opened the top. The heavy top sat back on its hinges exposing its contents. The refreshing smell of cedar filled the air. Where once it had held sheets, pillowcases, and blankets to be used by the young bride, it now swelled with invaluable mementos of war, weddings, and wishes. There were locks of grandchildren's first growth of hair; baptismal, First Communion, and wedding dresses; faded, dried corsages; pictures of my dad in his military uniform; and even a few of the tiniest teeth in an envelope.

Mom sat back in the chair and looked away, as if to avoid seeing. In the next second, she leaned forward to view the contents. A wistful—almost sad—look crossed her face. Her wrinkled, unsteady hand reached in. Her arthritic, knobby fingers ran across the white netting covering the smooth satin of her wedding gown. She wanted to touch, to hold as much as she could. Few words were spoken. Her eyes and facial expressions did the communicating.

Then it was time to return any contents to the chest for safekeeping. I carefully closed the chest's top. It was silent except for the click of the latch as it shut tightly.

I turned to Mom. Her head was bowed as in reverence to a sacred event that had just taken place. Her eyes brimmed with tears.

"What's wrong, Mom?" I asked.

"Oh, I don't know," she uttered. "I just feel so sad that my time has gone so quickly."

Having become somewhat impatient, I proceeded to lecture my mom on her negativity, to tell her that she had much time left. She didn't say a word in response.

With that, we began our descent down Everest.

Now, and only now, do I fully understand the rationale and gravity of our excursion to open the cedar chest. Mom had beaten death when she survived her stroke. She was fast approaching her nineties. She needed to review her life, to remember who she was and where she had been before.

A second, lasting memory took place the winter before Mom passed. My dad had died. Mom lost her incentive and was not ambulatory anymore. My sister and I both needed to continue working, and constant home care was far too expensive for our means. So, Mom entered a small, well-run nursing facility. My sister and I took turns visiting Mom every single day, including weekends. On my weekday visits, I would stay at my job doing reports and planning until dinnertime. Then, I would proceed to the nursing home and be with, Mom while she ate her dinner.

On one such night, the winter air was brutally cold. Snow was on the ground, and the wind was fierce and sharp. I arrived at the facility with red cheeks and numb hands. My mom was sitting up in her bed waiting for me. Her wrinkled, gnarled, and arthritic hands were resting on top of her blanket.

She took one look at me and said, "Come here." She motioned me to sit next to her on the bed, and I did. She then lifted up the blanket and told me to put my hands under it. I did, and she covered them. She then placed her hands over the blanket covering mine. She looked straight at me with tears in her eyes. She spoke, "My poor little girl," she muttered.

I was into my early sixties at that point, but I knew her daughters would always be, Mom's little girls. She was always the devoted, loving, maternal mother.

* * * * *

Dad

In order to fully portray my dad, I must first write of the man who raised him, the patriarch of the paternal side of my family. For my dad inherited much of who his own dad had been.

My dad's father emigrated from Italy as a very young husband and father. He was a man of slight stature and build. When he arrived in this country, my grandfather was not unlike most immigrants at the time. He couldn't speak English, he didn't have any specific skills, and he had little to no savings. Yet he was a proud man. He had a strong, decent character, a driving desire to succeed, and the will to become an American citizen. He would eventually begin working in a local factory as did so many immigrants at this time. And as was the case, unfortunately, with so many like him, his job often consisted of extremely difficult work. Such work was given to my grandfather even though he was the smallest man on the crew, and he knew why. He was an immigrant. He could not always be understood when he spoke nor could he always understand when spoken to. Yet my grandfather, so like my own dad, rarely complained.

He awoke at the crack of dawn every morning. His breakfast consisted of black coffee with a shot of whiskey in it and a biscotti. He then would put on his only blazer-type jacket and head on foot all the way across town to the factory. If it rained or snowed, he put bags over his shoes. He had no boots. I would recall this years later when my mom told me about my own dad. She recalled how he wore shoes with numerous holes in the bottom because he couldn't afford new shoes. Like father, like son.

My grandfather stayed with that job for years until his retirement. That job was sacred to him and he wasn't going to lose it.

Eventually, Grandfather, lovingly called Papanon by his grandkids, would purchase a one-family home. His chest swelled with pride. That home, even in later years, exuded warmth and love when one entered it. It was the cocoon that sheltered and nurtured a family of achievement. It remains in the paternal side of the family to this day.

Indeed, my dad was a carbon copy of his father in so many ways. Dad, too, was short in stature and of slight build. Yet was, and remains, the strongest man I have ever known. Dad could be very stubborn. He was a man of steel when it involved his convictions and determination. What Dad believed in was what he lived. Fortunately, he believed in the right things, such as family values, loyalty, forgiveness, hard work, responsibility, and the list goes on ad infinitum.

On many an occasion, my sister and I have bemoaned the fact that we always honor our commitments even when sick as a dog. Responsibility, loyalty, work…of course, we blame Dad for this!

My dad graduated high school but didn't have the finances to even entertain thoughts of college. Nevertheless, Dad had a great business mind and established a small grocery store soon after high school graduation. His time there would be short-lived. Soon, he would become a soldier as war loomed over our country. In his absence, his sister would man the store. Later, another family member would become a partner.

When Dad returned from the war, he went back to building his business, even peddling goods on the road. At age thirty, he married my mom and eventually became a father.

Dad wanted to build his dream home—a brick English Tudor with beautifully landscaped grounds. He didn't have the money for such an undertaking, but once again, his determination won. He would build that house, literally brick by brick, board by board. On Sunday afternoons (his only free time), he would work on the house until later in the evening. My mother's frustration would build as she waited for one room after another to be completed. It was a long haul. It took years.

When the house was completed, it *was* Dad's dream home. To this very day, his mark is everywhere in that home, and I continue to take great pride in the fact that I handed him stones as he built the beautiful wall around the house. (I need to note here, however, that as a five-year-old helper, I drove him crazy with incessant talking.)

Dad was able to build his business successfully, provide well for his family, and deal with the inevitable ups and downs of life. He did this like everything else he did—with determination, unbelievable patience, and ignoring idiots. He was a quiet man of resolve. During one of the more trying times in our family, he said, "No one is going to ruin this family." And they didn't.

Dad never had a vacation or a "good rest," as he called it. He continued to work at the store well into his later years. Some people berated him for this. My dad ignored them. He continued to do what he loved—being with people and being productive.

When not at the store, he worked his other job, which was caring for our mother. She had suffered a stroke. Mom's physical limitations, combined with her unwavering, steel-strong personality, presented quite a challenge—even for Dad. My sister and I did all we could, but then returned to our own homes and responsibilities. Dad never got that respite.

Within a short period of time, Dad became quite frail himself. He experienced a few falls. He was approaching his eighty-eighth birthday.

Early that summer, Dad was diagnosed as having a hernia. It needed to be surgically repaired. He entered the hospital and had a successful surgery the following day, but within a few days, he developed pneumonia. He passed away less than twenty-four hours later. It was July 4. *How fitting was that for such a patriotic, hardworking American?* I thought.

Mom would follow Dad a short time later.

* * * * *

Memories

I smell Sunday breakfast cooking downstairs. The wonderful smells waft up the stairs to my room. I breathe in the fresh-brewed coffee, sizzling bacon, and frying eggs.

Now I am running down the stairs at top speed. Occasionally, I jump onto the brass railing and slide to the bottom of the stairs, much to my poor father's horror. If it is summer, I awaken to the heavenly smells of a variety of roses growing in the rose garden. Yes, the smells of my childhood remain so vivid, a constant in my early life and home. But smells are not the only nostalgia surrounding me in this soon-to-be-empty home. Sounds are very much a part of this, too.

Our family's parish church is one street over from our home. It rests on top of a small hill at the end of that street. Its beautiful brick steeple can be seen from our home. In fact, when the original church burned, my father purchased many of its bricks to help build our home. The connection to the church is a deep one for me. I believe that my love of the movie *The Bells of St. Mary's* comes from this connection. Our church's name is St. Mary's.

Ah yes, the sound of those church bells playing a beautiful hymn or seasonal carol can still be heard in my mind. It is just as clear as the fire whistle that blew loud and clear throughout my town every evening at nine o'clock sharp, announcing the since-eliminated town curfew. The whistle of the commuter train pulling into the college station remains a sound fixture as well. But the best sounds come from Mom and Dad: my dad's voice announcing his arrival home as he opened the back door or my mom yelling at the bottom of the stairs the proverbial, "Snow day, no school!" Ah, those words were sweetness to my young schoolgirl ears. Sights, sounds, smells…memories everlasting. Now to empty the physical contents.

Cleaning, Emptying, Disposing

A friend of mine told me once about inheriting the daunting job of cleaning out her family home. The attic, as in most cases, became the "hellhole" where her parents stored years upon years (fifty, to be exact) of children's belongings, seasonal decorations, and the inevitable mountains of paper. In fact, every single receipt, bill, correspondence, etc., ever received was kept right up there in the attic. Sound familiar? Five (yes, five!) truckloads of paper were eventually carried away. In any case, cleaning out a home well-lived in is both daunting and exhausting, not to mention the emotional side of the task.

My wonderful, courageous sister was the designated person who cleaned out our family home. She and her husband were the last to live there after our parents were gone. She assumed the responsibility with no objections from the rest of us, which consisted of me and my three children. Being the saint she truly is, she handed down "must-be-kept" items to the appropriate individuals. She made countless trips to my home to offer items, and she donated many items to deserving organizations.

My sister had always been the strong, sensible, stoic type. Silently, I marveled at her strength in sorting through and relinquishing our family's treasure trove. It wasn't until the day that she and her husband were leaving to relocate to a warmer, friendlier climate that the real truth came out. She arrived at my house, carrying one last box of items. As she set them down, she turned to me with tears in her eyes and said, "Don't ever move from your house. It is just too difficult." We kissed and said our goodbyes.

Going Back

My core family's musical had ended. The creators of that musical no longer existed in this world. My only sibling had moved far away.

By the same token, my children were now grown and were building their lives away from home. My musical had also completed its run.

I had just retired from my life's work. I felt "lost."

It was "me, myself, and I." My husband was as supportive as he could be, but this was something I had to work through myself. There were "unsettled" feelings within me. I couldn't tell what those "unsettled" things were, but they were there. I needed to review my life, to attempt to discover what made me tick, and to find the core of who I was.

* * * * *

My earliest years were happy. I had a loving family and a secure home. I was protected—almost sheltered. Goodness and love were all around.

My parents married at thirty, which was considered "older" for that time. They were secure in themselves. They treated everyone with fairness and kindness. Because of where I came from, I thought everyone was like them. Surprise!

My initial thrust into the real world was when I started school. Even at such a young age, I was a very pensive child—a deep thinker. I was taught to be extremely polite. I was told that one went to school to learn and, also, to make friends. Boy, was I blindsided.

In school, there were some children who were bullies. (Isn't it strange how bullies survive the test of time?) I, of course, was the original poster child for these bullies. I didn't know how to fight back, either physically or verbally. This difficulty would follow me for a great part of my life. I was fine in the classroom but dreaded good ol' recess, where I became a moving target.

When the school day ended, I couldn't get home fast enough. My mom was there to soothe me with comforting words and food. However wonderful this was, it didn't teach me how to cope with people in the real world. I had learned well from my parents, and boy, was I paying the price!

The brazen kids at school were not the only bullies. Adults can be bullies too. I vividly recall one of my mother's in-laws. I can't bring myself to call her aunt. That would be far too kind. Now I realize she was a jealous, angry woman who used sarcasm and putdowns to attempt to make others feel inferior. I believe she knew no other way. I was the type of person she loved to intimidate, so I received the brunt of her self-hatred. Before she would arrive at our house, my mother would say, "Be good girls." Thus we accepted this admonishment as keeping our mouths shut as "good" girls should.

Surprisingly, I managed to get through grade school and junior high with high academic achievement and a cluster of friends. I remained fairly conservative and very quiet. The bullying and slights definitely impacted my self-image, however, and made me become a people pleaser. I desperately wanted to fit in.

By the time I started high school, I was able to find somewhat of a niche. I did well academically, became involved in numerous activities, and dated. At the end of my sophomore year of high school, I began dating a boy who was a year older. I liked everything about him and believed he felt the same. We spent countless hours together over the next four years. We attended school activities together. We dated every weekend and vacation. He spent many hours at my home. We were inseparable.

When we went to college, we wrote to one another nearly every day. We vowed our devotion to one another. I believed we would always be together. There was only one problem. Actually, there were a number of problems. Because of who I was—and that included my overriding naiveté—I never saw what was right in front of me. I never acknowledged the putdowns that were slid into our conversations. I never allowed myself to think about the totally different way he was raised. After much time, I came to see clearly that underneath that innocent look was a bully not unlike those who tormented me and others in grade school and beyond. To say that I was taken on a long, emotional ride is quite an understatement.

The relationship ended abruptly and nastily during the summer between my freshman and sophomore years of college. I was devastated. Now my perception of myself took a dive. I had no self-confidence left. I wanted to go away and just disappear. Young first love can do that to a fragile-minded individual. It can either be a pleasant lifelong memory or one that will always leave a bad taste in one's mouth. Soon, anger was added to insecurity, and I wasted precious time, chastising myself for my horrible judgment. Fortunately, I would soon have to return to college. Unaware to me, I would then begin a pattern that would become a go-to for me for the greater part of my life.

My Go-To

I returned to college that fall and threw myself into my studies and college life. I joined as many activities as I possibly could without jeopardizing my studies. I joined a service sorority. I continued to see my wonderful college friends on the weekends, and I dated. It was all part of my "college immersion"— my escape from bad memories and nasty people in my past. The lengths to which I threw myself into activity was a mere avoidance, but I didn't know it. I had just filed away one of my first losses in a folder marked "Loss," threw it into the cabinet of my mind, and slammed the door shut. The end.

The remainder of college flew by in a flash. I graduated and returned home for the summer. I had secured a job in my field at a state facility nearby, but it was only a summer position. I had barely settled into the job when I heard about a full-time open-ing in a school system close to home. I immediately applied and would be given the position. This would be my first full-time job in my profession.

On the first day of work, I parked my car and nervously walked across the parking lot to the school. As I approached the building, I saw a man standing on the sidewalk. He appeared to be waiting for me. As I came closer, he stuck out his hand to greet me. He had an honest face and a strong, firm handshake. He smiled and said, "I know who you are because you're the only new personnel here this summer." Little did I know but I had just met my future husband.

* * * * *

I loved my job and met several wonderful people there. The man who had waited for me on the sidewalk went out of his way to speak with me every day. By the end of six weeks, we had started to date. It was a wonderful time in my life, and it was going to get even better. By Christmastime, we were engaged.

We planned a spring wedding. Between my full-time job and the ongoing wedding preparations, I barely had time to think. I was more than ready for the journey. I would cherish every step.

We married on a beautiful sunny day in early spring. It had snowed a little the night before, which is not unusual in early spring, but I was prepared for a cold, windy wedding day. Surprise! The next day dawned with bright sun, clear blue sky, and warmer temperatures. I saw this as an omen of my married future.

We settled into married life with ease. We enjoyed purchasing our first home and planning the redo. I continued to work for nearly four years until our first child was born. She was beautiful—skin like porcelain, violet-blue eyes, and strawberry blond hair. She was her father's daughter. She was doted on by everyone in our family. Within two years, she had to share the spotlight with a sibling. A third sibling followed three years later.

By now, our home was bursting at the seams. More work was done to accommodate our growing brood. Everyone was healthy and thriving. At this point, I had my hands full as a full-time, stay-at-home mom. Life was exactly how I imagined it should be. To me, everything was perfect.

I now know full well that "perfect" doesn't last forever. I didn't know it then.

Spiraling Downward

One morning, four years after my oldest daughter's birth, while cleaning the den, I suddenly stopped to listen to a TV interview taking place. The interviewee was a pediatric specialist from the then Joslin Diabetes Center in Boston. He was speaking about Type 1 diabetes—also known as juvenile or insulin-dependent diabetes.

As I listened, a wave of anxiety hit me. A feeling of dread spread through my body. But why? I rationalized that it could be because my maternal grandmother had Type 1 diabetes. She took insulin shots daily. Due to this, my mom had educated us on the signs of diabetes. Mom would tell us that Type 1 diabetes often skipped a generation before attacking another family member. In any case, I felt frozen. My anxiety mounted, but I couldn't rationalize why. I would find out before too long.

* * * * *

It was the day of our ninth wedding anniversary. My husband and I planned an evening out. We had been looking forward to this for a while. My mom and sister would sit with the kids. It was a fairly typical day, but as it wore on, I began having concerns over our oldest child. In fact, I had noticed over the last several days that she was increasingly thirsty. She had also developed a ravenous appetite, as opposed to her usual "picky" one. As her dinner hour approached, she became irritable and kept asking for drink and food. When she finally sat down with her siblings for dinner, she "inhaled" seven glasses of liquid as well as a full meal!

Then I took a long, hard look at her. I could no longer pretend not to see what was in front of me. For all her drinking and eating over the previous week or so, my daughter was pale, her beautiful, large eyes were hollow, and her clothes hung on her. I could hear my heart beating, then racing.

My husband had returned home from school. He was a science teacher at middle and high school levels. Crazy as it sounds, that week he had been teaching about blood levels and how to test for diabetes and other related problems. For some reason which evades me now, he had brought home the testing equipment. It was in his desk drawer.

I spoke to my husband about my concerns for our daughter. He, of course, thought I was overreacting but said he would test her urine to allay my fears. It was now six o'clock. The two oldest girls were playing with dolls on the playroom floor. My husband went into the bathroom with the test kit. I had collected a small vial of urine for him to test. Minutes passed. It seemed like hours. My mom and sister arrived to babysit.

Finally, my husband opened the bathroom door. Tears were streaming down his face. In his hand, he held a test tube containing my daughter's urine. The urine was the brightest orange. We both knew what that meant. Our precious four year old was a Type 1 diabetic. This would be her "new normal," but for us, nothing would be normal again.

I froze. My mom and sister turned pale. My thoughts raced. How could this be? Why her? Why now? Why? Why? Why? No answers came but one thing was certain: My perfect life had just begun its downward spiral.

In an instant we—me, my husband, and my daughter—were on our way to the closest hospital. The doctor on call had told us over the phone that my daughter mustn't fall asleep. If that was to happen, in all likelihood, she wouldn't wake up.

In the backseat, I held my daughter and the doll she had been playing with. That night, she had her first night away from us. The very next day, she would be transported to the Joslin Diabetes Center, the same facility that had treated her great-grandmother so many years before. I stayed in Boston to be with my child. I would attend lectures and classes to learn about Type 1 diabetes and how to learn to live with a child having it. She would also attend classes with children her age.

That week was more than tough. I needed to be there, but I missed and worried about my three year old and one year old. I also missed my husband terribly. I relied on him so much. I was afraid to speak up when needed. I was frightened of the whole situation. Why did I have to be alone? Where was God in all this? Any parent having a child diagnosed with a life-threatening illness will say the same thing: The child as you knew her or him is gone. You just mourn that loss and face the "new" child.

One night at the hospital, I was giving my child a bath. I looked at her little body so emaciated, her skin white, her eyes sunken. I shuddered. She stared back at me. She must have read my thoughts because she quietly said, "Mama, I can't help the way I look. God made me this way." And so He had. She was perfect in body and soul.

That evening, after having tucked her into bed, I began a ritual that I would repeat every evening until we left the hospital. I would walk the long corridor connecting the hospital wings, repeatedly muttering to myself. "She will have a normal life if it kills me." It almost did.

My daughter and I had been thrust into learning as much as we could at the hospital. I wanted to sell our home and move into an apartment across from the hospital, but neither the doctors nor my husband thought it a good idea. So now we were going home, home to attempt to recreate a semblance of normalcy for everyone in our family while attempting to keep our daughter well.

Back Home

After returning home from the hospital, the following months were trying for all of us. We struggled to comprehend our child's illness and all that it encompassed. This included ongoing blood testing, giving multiple insulin shots, and logging data on blood sugar levels and reactions. Special meals and snacks had to be prepared for our four-year-old as well. In addition to this, my husband was attempting to build a new business to support our family.

Once again, I called upon the protective protocol I had established after my earlier losses. I threw myself into overdrive. The heartache, anxiety, and anger were somewhere in another file marked "Loss" and locked away. I worked like a whirling dervish. I scrubbed and cooked relentlessly. I played with the children and did projects. In the evening, I fell asleep, exhausted, before repeating my method of operation the next day.

July passed and we celebrated our youngest daughter's first birthday. It was nice to have something positive to plan.

August began on a good note. We worked and played in the yard. Our oldest had many playdates, and we were beginning to establish a modicum of normalcy. August 10 was a Sunday. It was a bright, beautiful late summer's day. We had invited a couple we met at the Joslin Center to come over for a cookout. In the early morning, my husband, who now ran an antiques business, received a call from an older woman he knew who sold antiques. She wished to sell him some things. He agreed to see her. My husband was gone for several hours. When he returned, he had purchased numerous items, many of which were useless to him for resale.

"Why did you buy these?" I asked.

His response? "She is very ill and desperately needs money."

Cream rises to the top. Amen. We then prepared for our company. I dressed the girls in their prettiest summer frocks. I dressed up a bit, too. I walked outside with the children. We joined hands and walked across the yard to the old wall to look for chipmunks. Their dad was grilling. His eyes followed us as we walked down and back. As we approached him, he said to me, "You look just like the day I married you. I wish I had a picture of all of you to remember how you look right now."

I would like to believe that his mind's eye snapped that picture to store in his *eternal* memory.

Before long, our guests arrived and we settled down to good conversation and food. As the afternoon wore on, more people unexpectedly arrived. My parents decided to stop over, as did my husband's sister and her husband. Interestingly, my husband's sister lived at a distance and only happened to be in our area by chance: She had been given a gift certificate for a nearby restaurant and decided to use it *that* day. My husband was very close to his sister, so he was thrilled to see her. Later I would question if this was merely by chance or part of the Divine Plan.

All of us talked, laughed, and ate until later evening. It had been the best day of the summer thus far, and it seemed as though all of us were reluctant to see it come to an end.

The children were exhausted. We prepared them for bed and they quickly fell asleep. Because I was such an early riser, I turned in as well. My husband loved to stay up late. The house was quiet then. He would take a number of books down from the shelf and pore over them for hours.

In the wee hours of the morning, I heard a kind of "quickstep"—a running—through the living room. Our youngest daughter, who had just turned one, had been crying. My husband had picked her up and was rocking her. Just before this, he was feeling a tightening in his chest. It had been getting worse as he held the baby. He had put her down and was making a fast run to the kitchen phone.

"What's wrong?" I asked.

"I'm having chest pains," he said. "Call 911."

As I went to the phone, he ran to the den couch to lie down. When I got there, his eyes were rolling back and he was covered in a profuse sweat. Sweat was literally dripping off his face. But the next second, he had regained composure and was speaking to me.

Within minutes, the police arrived. At the time our town did not have its own ambulance; we shared one with a neighboring community. One of the policemen immediately called for the ambulance, but it was out on a run. We would have to wait.

Meanwhile, an officer checked my husband's blood pressure and then rushed into another room to make a call. I could hear him saying, "We need an ambulance immediately. Please make it quick." Minutes passed, five…ten…and the officer made another call for the ambulance.

I went to my husband's side. He was obviously in much distress. But he looked at me and half-convincingly said, "Nothing bad is going to happen because we are good people." I wish all that "goodness" did have such a prophecy with it, but so many of us know that reality doesn't always work that way.

My parents and sister were called to stay with the children who, miraculously, slept through all the activity. They arrived just as the ambulance pulled in.

In a mad rush, the EMTs carried in a stretcher, secured my husband on it, and proceeded to carry him out the side door. I was standing on the threshold to the den, watching this scenario with disbelief. Could this really be happening to me? To us? Why?

As I looked down at my husband being carried out, he turned and yelled to me, "Take care of those kids." His last paternal orders had been given. His last words as a husband and father had been spoken. I would recall those words again and again for the rest of my life. They were now a part of my being.

I followed the EMTs holding the stretcher outside. They told me I could ride with them. I jumped into the back of the ambulance. My husband's breathing was extremely labored. One could sense the pain and fight in him even after the oxygen mask was applied.

As the ambulance whisked through the streets, I recall looking at the dark, quiet neighborhoods, so peaceful. I recall thinking, "The world is at rest." I felt as if I were outside of this world and looking at a totally different one, like through a looking glass.

Finally, after what seemed to me to be an eternity, we arrived at the hospital. My husband was quickly brought into an emergency space. As the door closed, I saw nurses, doctors, and technicians surrounding him. My husband had suffered a very bad heart attack. I soon learned that a heart surgeon had been summoned to place a pacemaker in him.

My sister arrived and sat with me. Within a short period of time, a doctor and nurse entered the waiting room. I can still picture the pain on the nurse's face. I can still feel myself go numb. I can still hear myself ask, "How can I tell my children?"

Unfortunately, there are no scripts written for such life events.

My sister is a worldly saint. She was with me every step of the way. We walked into the room where my husband lay. I talked to him. Sound is supposed to be the last faculty to go. I recall exactly what I said. I believe he heard me.

* * * * *

Most individuals think of shock with negativity, but it really can be a "beautiful" thing. In the event of immeasurable loss or pain, it becomes an anesthesia putting one into a false state of existence. For that short period, one can walk, speak, and greet while feeling numb and "totally" lost. And so it was for me.

Nevertheless, the kids needed clean clothes. There were diapers to wash. But whenever I got to "his" shirts and socks, I couldn't bear to pick them up. They would have to wait.

The kids had to be fed. They needed baths. A good man, a wonderful husband, a very proud dad was gone, but his children were still very much alive. They were the part of him that was still here, and I intended to take "good care" of them, just as he had ordered.

The following days were trying to say the least. I was never alone so I didn't have time to dwell on the extent of my family's loss and the tremendous impact it would make for a long, long time. People would be coming and going with food and flowers. In the beginning, this was probably a good thing. The clergy came to check on us. Some individuals overstayed their welcome. Others freely gave of useless, insensitive advice.

Nonetheless, it probably was a good thing not to be totally alone. I found when I was alone, I literally wanted to climb the walls! Complete silences became my enemy. It was a very real dilemma that would last for weeks. I was in my own way and couldn't help myself. I was at an emotional impasse.

Yet I knew instinctively that my children needed me. Regardless of pain and anxiety, I needed to be "present." This was especially true with my oldest. I was still in the beginning stages of caring for her diabetes. Her dad had been the primary caregiver for her blood testing and insulin injections. One of his degrees was in microbiology. He was certainly more scientifically knowledgeable than I. Besides, our daughter trusted him beyond measure. On the other hand, I was very insecure about administering injections. What if I hurt her? What if she flinched? My daughter was well aware of my feelings and behavior. To make matters worse, this child was extremely strong-willed and verbal. She never hesitated to tell me when I was being a bumbling idiot.

In any case, I was forced to move through each day. Some days felt like they would never end. My body was moving, but my mind was constantly filled with troubling questions. There were years left in which to raise my children. Would I have the stamina to do this? How would I manage as both mother and father? Would I be capable of raising and caring for my child with a life-threatening illness? And what about money? My cash flow was zero at the time, and our savings nearly nonexistent. Remember, my husband had recently poured most of our savings into starting a new business. And because he had resigned from his teaching position just weeks before our daughter's illness, our health insurance had been canceled.

Author Lynn Caine, in her bestseller, *Widow*, ascertains that no matter how much money a widow has, she will constantly fret about finances. I was, and continue to be, no exception. To this day, I still count the money in my wallet every time I leave the house. Similarly, I am forever checking my bank balances.

So now, like Lynn Caine, I was a widow. Horrors! I detest that word as much now as I did then.

Carrying on

Soon it was fall. The oldest two children would be going off to school. A routine needed to be established. My oldest daughter started first grade and my middle daughter started nursery school. I realized I had to return to work very soon. I needed a job that would provide a steady income.

At first, I took any job I could find. My first job was as a preschool aide. I loved being around the kids, but the head teacher (who was also the owner) was a spoiled young woman who lots of her frustrations out on me. I become the official fanny and nose wiper. There was no way that she was ever going to utilize my background in language development and therapy. It was the job from hell, but I needed it.

Within a year's time, I moved from nursery school aide to public school aide, which would eventually land me my lasting job. But in the interim, I started working in another district for two different speech pathologists, both of them on maternity leave. It would be a short stint, but just what the doctor ordered. It felt terrific being back in my field. When I went to work, I was the "professional me"—not the "wife me" or "mother me," or worse, the "widow me."

I was just me! This job would come to an end after three months. I dreaded leaving. It was during my time there that I met a man who lived in my community. We met briefly one day in one of the school's offices. We had never met or seen each other before even though we lived in the same small community. I didn't know at the time, but his marriage had broken up. I confided in him about my husband. We seemed to have a lot in common and talked every day that I worked at the school. Then the job ended. The permanent staff returned, and I was back in financial limbo. I immediately began searching for new employment. Interestingly enough, my relationship with the individual from school didn't end. Not long after I left, he phoned me. He was going to attend a banquet and asked me to go along. I still had feelings of betrayal whenever I entertained the thought of dating. After all, I was the one who lived. I was the one who stayed home to care for the children while my husband worked long and hard to provide for us. Did I cause or contribute to his demise? So now add "blame" to my roster of feelings. I would learn that these feelings can be common to a widow or widower, and they weighed heavily on me.

At any rate, I agreed to go to the banquet. I rationalized that an evening out with a friend was innocent enough. The evening was fun, and he was a nice guy. He could understand feelings of loneliness, anxiety, and inadequacy. This would be the beginning of many dates.

While I was still actively looking for employment, I happened to haphazardly hear about a position in my field in the local school system. I immediately applied for the job. After a number of interviews, I was hired. I was going back to the place where my professional career had begun. I would be amid friends, and best of all, I would be within arm's length of my children during the day. Call it luck. I called it Divine Intervention. Life was very busy. Things were looking up.

Within two years, I would marry my current husband, the man I had met at my subbing job. The following ten to fifteen years would pass quickly in a flurry of activity. The children were deeply immersed in their studies, school and outside activities, and friendships.

My husband and I both taught full time in addition to carrying on our own individual activities and pursuits. Added to all of this was the adjustment to a new family configuration. As most reconstructed families can attest, this can be extremely daunting, but we muddled through as most do.

My children were very close in age. For this reason, they followed closely behind each other in middle and high school. Once in high school, the years flew by rapidly. There were dates, proms, more outside activities, and visiting; and applying to colleges. They would soon be leaving the nest. For some parents, this would be a blessing—a respite from the trying teenage years of needing to be constantly present to monitor the carefree, often outlandish behavior of the teenager. This need for a break between parent and child is understandable in many cases.

For me, it was the opposite, perhaps, because I needed my children almost more than they needed me. I loved being involved in so much of what they did, and how much they accomplished. Perhaps, it was because they were pieces of their Dad that I wanted to cling to. Letting go was like losing my primary identity, my valuable self—being a mother to my kids.

It was hard enough letting go of my oldest daughter, but I still had two others ta home. The day my second child left for college is the one I will never forget. As she stood in the doorway of her dorm room to say goodbye, I looked at her and so many moments throughout the years with each of my daughters flashed by in an instant. The handwriting, as they say was on the wall. Soon, I would have an empty nest. What would the rest of my journey be like?

Interestingly, just as my children left home and needed me less and less, my parents needed me and my sister more and more. They had become quite elderly. My dad passed on first. Soon after, my mom needed to go into a nursing home. Between work and visits to Mom, time managed to pass quickly despite my empty nest.

I also had time to do more reading, thinking, and contemplating new things.

It was now well into the 1990s, paranormal events became a favorite topic, particularly among the

New Age population. "Spirituality" was a common word, as was the phrase "Near Death Experience." The latter expression was a phenomenon that people had been interested in and had speculated about for as long as humanity existed.

For whatever reason, I developed an "uncanny" thirst for NDEs (near death experiences). I read anything and everything on this topic that I could get my hands on. Fortunately, new material on this topic was being published almost monthly. Two trailblazers in this area were Dr. Melvin Morse, MD, and Dr. Raymond Moody, MD. Drs. Morse and Moody, in addition to others, documented these experiences in children and adults who were near or at the point of being clinically dead. Because modern medicine now had the means to revive many who were clinically dead, increasing numbers of NDEs were told and documented.

Dr. Morse, a pediatrician, studied children—many very young—who supposedly were revived after having died. In his book, *Closer to the Light*, he tells the stories relayed by his young patients. He describes their stories as being vivid, highly detailed, and amazingly told in language not found in children their age. He states that such stories couldn't possibly have been made up.

Yet despite such concrete research and data, huge numbers of people found NDEs hard to accept. Unfortunately, skepticism is still found today after monumental data has been collected. The irony in this is that NDEs have been reported throughout the ages. Some accounts involve Native American leaders, such as Black Elk. Others involve Indian gurus like Paramahansa Yogananda. The latter described his NDE in a book he wrote titled, *Autobiography of a Yogi*.

Among others documenting NDEs were Calvinist theologian Jonathan Edwards and the Oxford scholar Edward Robinson. Robinson reported having had a spiritual, paranormal experience at age four. Both Edwards and Robinson made reference to the "Light," which is found throughout the Bible as well.

In more modern times, including up to the present, naysayers argue that such experiences are merely hallucinations resulting from drug-taking or psychological disorders. Scientific research conducted in hospitals and independent labs seeks to dispel such beliefs. Documentation from random groups of drug users is heavily relied upon and the drugs involved include a wide variety of types. Such drugs include LSD, morphine, heroin, PCP, cocaine, marijuana, and barbiturates, to mention a few.

From this expanse of research came the following commonalities. Those involved in the research describe feelings of absolute tiredness, poor visual field, nausea and vomiting, and an inability to concentrate and perform. Some hallucinatory behavior was noted. However, none of these findings compared in any way, shape, or form to a near death experience. Only those experiencing NDEs exhibit being detached from the body but still having consciousness.

One more aspect of my reading touched a chord in me. All of the reports I read ended with the same thing—that those who truly experience NDEs continued to experience paranormal psychic phenomena throughout their remaining lives. These phenomena included problems with watches or timepieces worn on the body; precognitive hunches, visions, and occasional acute smells indicating a presence or coming event.

This information made my hair stand on end. Why was it that I had a drawer full of watches—many brand-new—that stopped working for no reason? They would have new batteries installed to no avail.

By the same token, I recalled dreams just before my daughter became ill and just prior to my first husband's death. Both were vivid dreams in which sickness appeared to be the foreboding message. The first dream occurred months before my eldest daughter was diagnosed as a type 1 diabetic. In the dream, she and her middle sister were sitting at a picnic table. My younger daughter was smiling and laughing. My older daughter was looking directly at me. She looked very sad and sick. She appeared to be bloated, and her face looked scared. In a few months, she would become ill.

The second, foreboding dream took place within a few short weeks of my husband's death. In that dream, the vision was only from his shoulders up. He was wearing the new gray suit that he had recently purchased for a school reunion. It was the suit he was buried in. In the dream, he appeared to be looking off in the distance. What was startling to me was that a cloud of smoky gray enveloped the back and sides of this vision. The dream bothered me then, as it still does now.

There is no way I can reconcile myself to the fact that these dreams were just dreams. They were premonitions, for sure. Smells have also been a recurring phenomenon to me. On one such occasion, I experienced a strong, lasting smell of lavender. Experts in the psychic arena note, that such a smell is the hallmark of psychic experience. On still another such occasion, I awoke to a penetrating odor of rubbing alcohol. This disturbed me because of its possible implication of a doctor's office or a hospital, in fact, that's just what happened. Within a week, I found out I needed two medical procedures, including a biopsy and some surgery. Fortunately, both turned out fine, but had the possibility of being serious.

I have on at least two occasions smelled the lovely scent of roses when there were absolutely no roses present. This took place in a church and, as a Catholic, is believed to be the presence of the Blessed Mother Mary.

And don't forget my reaction years earlier when my heart felt like it stopped beating as I listened to a TV interview on Type 1 diabetes, later to learn that my daughter had it.

I recall many occasions when an individual not seen or mentioned in years would pop into my head, and shortly thereafter, I would run into them in the least likely place or get a call or card from them or learned that they had passed. One precognitive event took place the day before my dad's death. My dad had been in the hospital a few days for some minor surgery. The surgery turned out fine, but a few days later he developed what the doctor called "a little pneumonia." When we were notified of this by his doctor, my sister, her husband, and my mom were all present at my mom's home. I relayed the news, and as I did, the time 3:00 a.m. flashed across my mind much like a digital clock would. At 3:00 a.m. the next morning, my phone rang. My dad had died.

I could not reconcile that these precognitive events were merely by chance. They had been far too consistent for the past forty years or so to just be a coincidence. Why was I experiencing these phenomena? What had caused this? At the exact time and place, the answers would be revealed to me.

Journeying Back into the Past Leads to a Startling Revelation

I was engaged to my first husband during the 1971 Christmas season. It was an exciting time for both of us. We were invited to many social events by friends and family. One such event was hosted by a couple my future husband had known for a while. I had just met them in the fall. I recall that when I initially met them, the husband made me feel uneasy. I couldn't tell you why, but the feeling was there from our first meeting.

The night of the couple's party arrived. We were greeted by the wife at the door. There were many people there. We were soon ushered into a room where a bar was set up. The server was the husband. He had a flat affect and still made me very uncomfortable.

My fiancé and I began to mingle with other guests. He poured me a glass of cola as I requested. Before I had finished half of the cola, I began to feel strange. Very strange. I felt lightheaded. I recall quickly excusing myself and heading for the ladies room. Once inside, I lost what I would describe as "normal" consciousness. I clearly recall that I experienced a different kind of awareness. I remember being enveloped in a complete darkness and thinking, "I am dying." I began to beg God to let me live. Yet I wasn't hysterical. Even in that darkest of moments, I leaned on God and asked Him for help.

When a train goes through
a tunnel and it gets dark,

You don't throw away the
ticket and jump off.

You sit still and trust the
engineer.
—Corrie Ten Boom
Everyday Grace

Then, in what seemed like an instant, I was hovering above a card game in progress in another room. The male host was cheating, as was the individual next to him. I "perceived" that they had a game plan between them, though words were never spoken. Then total blackness again.

In the next instant (like turning to another channel on TV), I was standing by a body of water. The water wasn't moving, however. It was still. To my left was a figure. I never saw the face because a hood hung over the figure's forehead and covered the sides of the face. Yet I instinctively knew it was a man. He was attired in a robe-like garment and, as stated, a hood. In his right hand was what I would describe as a shepherd's hook or staff. Not a word was ever spoken to me but I was not afraid.

On the opposite side of the still water were trees and plants, similar to a wood or forest. The colors were varied but muted, not unlike a Monet painting. The figure and I merely stood there and looked, but in an instant, we were standing in a lower area which appeared to be at the end of a wooded path. There was a clearing of some distance ahead of us. We looked straight ahead. Off in that far distance was a high hill. On top of that hill was what can only be described as a magnificent castle. Yet the words "magnificent" and "castle" truly do not do it justice. It was huge and appeared to spread out on either side. From that structure emanated the most all-encompassing light one could ever imagine. The structure "glowed" and the light appeared to send out rays from every side.

After nearly forty-nine years I can still clearly see that amazing sight.

As we looked at this scene, the figure pointed straight ahead with his index finger. I perceived the thought, "There. Do you see it?" or "Do you wish to go there?" Then, blackout again.

To this very day, I do not know how long I was removed from reality. I was told it was a goodly amount of time. When I fully gained consciousness, my fiancé was sitting next to me. I was told that I had vomited just prior to coming to. My fiancé drove me home. I went straight to bed. The next day was strange. I felt strange to myself, maybe the way an astronaut feels upon returning to earth after a ride into space. I spent the following two days on the couch, resting. It took a few days before I felt like my old self. As was my fashion, I marked another of my mind's file folders, "What happened to me?", threw it in my mind's vault, and slammed the door shut. It would be some thirty years before I would think about that night again.

Can Angels Have Fur?

It was the fall of 2015 and a new phase in my life. My children were grown and very busy with their own demanding professions and personal lives. My husband and I retired from our jobs within months of each other. I had planned to carry on my work as a speech pathologist in the private sector, which I did.

I fully enjoyed every minute of doing private work. This would last for eight years.

During this period, our remaining pets passed on due, for the most part, to old age. Our family had always had pets. We were animal lovers in the truest sense of the word.

With the children and pets gone, we decided to adopt a new pet or two. So we headed for the local shelter, where we ended up adopting three beautiful felines. Two were a mother and daughter. The third, a huge French Blue, we named Bleu.

The daughter kitten, a mere runt, was never more than a foot away from her mother. The mama cat's name was Maddie, short for Madeleine. Maddie was a small girl herself with the softest grey and white fur. Her paws were the smallest I've ever seen, and her eyes were gorgeous.

Maddie loved to snuggle. She would snuggle with anyone for hours. My private students adored her. When I was working with a student, Maddie's favorite thing to do was to climb into that student's backpack and rest there until the student was leaving. People would constantly comment, "If only I had a cat like Maddie."

Yes, Maddie was special. You could tell that she had had a tough go of it. A torn ear certainly represented some distress at a point in her life.

We were told by the shelter personnel that Maddie had struggled to survive for herself and her kitten. They had been captured by the shelter workers attempting to climb the side of a large office building to get food the workers were offering from a window.

Maddie's personality was priceless. She could be cuddly and playful one minute, while in the next hissing and batting at other cats. And so Maddie fully and lovingly ingrained herself in us.

Nothing was too good for my pets. They were indoor cats and adjusted exceedingly well. In fact, my greatest fear was that one of my pets might escape outdoors and be lost to me forever.

* * * * *

It was Labor Day. The day had dawned bright and sunny. I was feeling bored and restless. I decided to go for a walk. Years before, I would walk with one of my precious cats in a stroller specifically designed for pets. It had netting enclosure on all sides and was perfectly secure. I felt comfortable doing this. That particular pet loved being in it. The stroller had subsequently been retired to the loft in our garage.

On this Labor Day, my husband was busy working in the yard. He insisted I take one of the cats with me in the old stroller. I told him the cats were scared of the outdoors and it wasn't a good idea. My husband nevertheless insisted. The next thing I knew, he had gone into the house and carried Maddie out. She looked petrified. He got the stroller down and placed her inside. She was zipped in. We both checked the enclosure multiple times, and it seemed perfectly fine.

I crossed our street and walked about five feet or so. Maddie was howling. Because my street is adjacent to a very busy highway, many trucks as well as other large vehicles utilize the street as a quick crossover to the highway.

I knew Maddie was petrified so I decided to cross over to the other side of the street and go home. Just as I did, the howling stopped. I figured Maddie had given up the howling and was complacently sitting down. So I stopped and looked inside.

She was gone! I felt faint. It was as if every inch of my body were paralyzed. I heard myself repeatedly saying aloud, "I can't do this." Off in the distant woods, I heard a faint "Meow"—the last ever from Maddie. I stood in that spot for I don't know how long.

In the days and weeks to come, I would post missing signs everywhere. I searched with family and wonderful friends. I notified police, veterinarian offices, and shelters—even our local bus drivers, who, in turn, asked their "riders" to help. As a final, concerted effort I placed a picture, with a large reward, in the newspaper. I even hired professional searchers from another state to look for my lost "girl." This started out well but did not end up with positive results. Maddie would never be found.

As is often the case, some individuals totally understood the bond I shared with my animal companions while others were one step away from being thoughtless. I would hear, "What's wrong with you?

It's only a cat," or "Go get another one right now and forget the whole thing." And on and on.

These comments reverberated within me. They unfortunately reminded me of hurtful comments made to me right after my first husband passed. "No one will marry you with three small children," or "I have told so many people about your home because you'll have to sell quickly. You can't afford to keep it."

I think the comment that hurt me the most, however, was made by an individual from the college town where I grew up. I ran into him one day a few months after my husband's death. I was still preoccupied with the loss and somewhat subdued. His comment to me? "It's hard to tell someone when they have emotional issues."

In retrospect, I wish I had retorted "And it's hard to tell someone when they are unfeeling and ignorant."

The insight I got from these "well meaning" individuals was to carefully weigh what I say to others who have suffered a loss—be it human or fur family member. Words are so powerful! They pack a punch few physical ones do.

* * * * *

Time continued to pass. Maddie hadn't been found. I wasn't sleeping well and I continued to cry. Not the usual cry, blow and wipe, and move on. I couldn't stop crying. It was a disaster when I needed to leave the house. I wore dark glasses inside and out whether sunny or pouring rain. When I did return to my home or car, I would sob, having had to hold back my flood of tears in public. My eyes became bright red and swollen. A few weeks into this, I had an appointment with my ophthalmologist for a checkup. He couldn't examine my eyes because of the condition they were in.

I was now physically and mentally spent. I lost my determination and my usual "get on with it" attitude. I felt like a failure and I didn't really know why. Most of the time, I wanted to die. It was getting too hard to live.

The Journey Begins

Despite my state of being, I was cognizant enough to realize I needed professional help. Someone once said that when you begin to cry at a sad movie, you then continue to cry for all the sad things in your life. In the book *Emotional Resilience* author David Viscott, MD, states that an "unexpected trigger" (e.g., a sad movie) awakens the old hurt/s "and grief returns once again. Viscott terms this "toxic nostalgia" (pp. 5–6).

I contacted a nearby counselor but that didn't work out. She needed her own counselor. Things were not getting better for me. The nights were the worst. I would sit and cry for hours.

One evening, my husband got up and went to his computer. When he returned, he handed me a piece of paper. On it was the name of a psychologist who specialized in grief counseling. Her name was Dr. Susan Berger. She had authored a wonderfully insightful book entitled *The Five Ways We Grieve*. I called the next day and set up an appointment.

The following week, I went to my first appointment with Dr. Berger. I liked her immediately. She was very professional but just as friendly and warm. I could instinctively tell that she cared.

Initially, my time in therapy centered around the loss of my beloved pet. Dr. Berger totally understood my feelings, being a devoted animal lover herself. She acknowledged my deep and sincere grief and allowed me all the time I needed to discuss and mourn my loss. A skilled counselor has the professional expertise to draw information out of a person—to dig deeper to expose the real issues and to help the individual bring to light how they feel, and why. Dr. Berger knew how to accomplish this.

For a while, I was unaware that my therapy sessions were bringing me closer and closer to my earliest past experiences. There were many questions that needed to be answered.

You may recall that my "mantra" had always been, "work, work, more work, so much to do, no time to dwell." I would file away these losses. Period.

Now, and only now, I had to face what was in those files. I had to face my demons. I had to realize that my feelings of unworthiness, rejection, loss, and failure had to be reckoned with.

It is virtually impossible to ever fully be aware of the amount of information stored within us. Deep in the recesses of the mind rest the childhood experiences, dreams, loves, dashed plans, grief, and the list goes on ad infinitum.

Perhaps the worst of all this is that one might never know which experience will set off a chain reaction of tidal wave proportions like I felt at the loss of Maddie.

As my therapy continued, I learned that with each new loss in life one needs to revisit previous losses to gain understanding and acceptance. How was each loss handled or not handled? How did each experience impact your life? Was there self-blame for some experiences? Why? These questions loomed in front of me.

Facing these demons was extremely difficult.

One thing I was certain of—I had blamed myself. When we blame ourselves, we find it almost impossible to forgive. It is so much easier to forgive others rather than ourselves. Maybe it is easier to blame ourselves because we feel the need to be punished. Yet in order to heal we must forgive—feel the pain and then peace. But I was the "Queen of Blame." I had even blamed myself for my daughter's illness. After all, it was my grandmother who had the diabetes. And my husband's death? Well, I had stayed home to be a full-time mom. If I had worked, I would have made things easier for us financially. He wouldn't have had to work so hard; he wouldn't have had a heart attack. He would have lived.

* * * * *

My time in therapy would last nearly two years. Under Dr. Berger's guidance, I had reopened my past. I had gained a commodity of self-acceptance.

I was on the road to making peace with myself. The fledgling now needed to leave the nest.

A very small, furry creature had led me to begin this journey. Perhaps angels can have fur after all.

Journey to The Soul

For some, the conclusion of therapy might have been the end of their soul-searching. For me, it wasn't. I wanted to know more about "me," and I felt strongly that there was more to know. Where to begin? Reading seemed a good place to start.

I soon learned there is no shortage of reading material on self-discovery, the psyche, and the paranormal.

I found that in the numerous books I read, the words "soul," "spirit," and "mind" were consistently used. The "soul" was most widely referred to. This intrigued me. So concentrating on the word "soul," I did.

As a Cradle Catholic, I was taught that the soul was the seat of salvation; *that it existed before birth and after death*; and that in life we needed to fight to save our soul by following the Ten Commandments—by living a good life and avoiding sin. Researching the soul presented with its own complexities, however. I found that the ancient Greeks were quite enthralled with what the soul was. The material passed down through the ages by them is impressive, proving once again that the Greeks were forerunners in this arena as in so many others.

Plato (428–348 BCE) initially referred to the subject of "the soul" as an immaterial concrete subject, but later referred to the soul as that which pre-exists the body and lives on after death.

The majority of the Greek philosophers agreed that whatever the soul was, it definitely was life-giving. For most of the philosophers this definition solely referred to humans.

It was Aristotle who suggested that there were "different souls"; that not only humans and animals had souls, but also plants. In other words, he maintained that all *living* things had a soul.

Aristotle stated that the soul in plants included the nutritive and reproductive (life-giving) powers. He suggested further that the human soul shared powers with the other living things but gave distinctive intellectual powers to humans.

The ancient Greeks were on to something, for in current literature, the worlds "soul" and "spirit" are often used interchangeably and in reference to both humans and animals. In addition, both words are found over eight hundred times in Scripture. Modern-day theorists, philosophers, and psychologists use very similar terminology in their definitions. One such individual, Yanki Tauber, stated on chabad.org that "the soul is the self, the 'I' that inhabits the body…without the soul, the body is like a lightbulb without electricity…with the introduction of the soul the body acquires life (spirit)."

The well-known Deepak Chopra refers to the soul as "the core of your being. It is eternal. It doesn't exist in space and time. It's a field of infinite creativity...your eternal reference point with which you should always be in touch."

Literature further indicates that the soul is what graces our being with spirit, creativity, and enlightenment. Each human being is unique and, therefore, it would make sense that each of our souls is unique as well.

The soul...where our life's journey begins... what makes our travels through life the ultimate personal experience containing the "ingredients" that make us who we are and, more importantly, who we are *capable of becoming*.

My research into the soul only strengthened my religious convictions—the beliefs taught to me from my birth as part of my "inherited" religion.

It was a gratifying realization.

One Last Startling Revelation

My family's home would soon be put up for sale. Much of the house had been cleaned of its furniture and decor. One day while at the house, I found myself heading up the stairs to my bedroom. I entered the room and stood there just to be "in the moment" and reminisce. I looked around, taking in every nook and cranny. I remembered the bright sun pouring in through the expanse of windows. I recalled the large, very beautiful picture of the Christ Child hanging on the wall. I saw my cozy bed under the dormer. And then in my mind's eye, I saw it!

To the right of my bed had once hung a small wrought-iron plaque. In the very center was the image of a little angel. The hands were folded as in prayer. Above the image, written in white letters, was the line: "The Lord is my shepherd…"

I gasped! I felt as if something had exploded in my head. My thoughts were spinning wildly. What was happening?

Then I began to mouth the words…

> *He leadeth me beside*
> *still waters…*
> *His rod and staff*
> *shall comfort me…*
> *He leadeth me through*
> *paths of righteousness…*

I clearly recalled the night of the Christmas party so many, many years before…being enveloped in darkness…having a "different" consciousness…a figure with a shepherd's hook to my left…then, still water…a path…finally, a "city of light." And for all time afterward, the premonitions, smells, broken watches, etc., I experienced.

For an instant, I was stunned but not for long. Soon my body was enveloped in warmth—the reaffirmation of not only having had a near death experience but realizing full well the magnitude of it. I had seen the "City of Light." The words that are referred to 440 times in the Bible Thesaurus. Specific references include:

Job 24:13
John 8:12
    3:16
    9:5

Matthew 5:13
    5:14
    5:16

Isaiah 60:1
Romans 13:11
    13:14

Ephesians 5:7
    5:14

Colossians 1:9
    1:14

Thessalonians 5:1
    5:11

Matthew 5:15 states:

> *Nor do people light a lamp*
> *and put it under a basket,*
> *but on a stand, and it gives*
> *light to all the house.*

In the King James version of the Bible, Isaiah 42:16 states:

> *I will lead (them)*
> *in paths (that) they have*
> *not known. I will make*
> *darkness light before them.*

Finally, Matthew 5:14:

> *You are the light of*
> *the world; a city set*
> *on a hill cannot be hidden.*

It is true. It is all true. I know because I witnessed it.

I believe now, though I didn't always, that our lives do have a plan that we are destined to follow.

I recently (February 9, 2018) read an article on the movie *The 15:17 to Paris*, in *The Pilot*, a Catholic newspaper. The movie revolves around a terrorist on a Paris-bound train. The terrorist was stopped by three young men who just happen to have the trained skills required to stop the terrorist. One is the son of a Baptist minister. The other two fellows have military training with guns, expertise in jiujitsu, and one as a medic. These credentials are perfect for obliterating the attack.

These young men believe that their presence on that train was no coincidence. All three believe that the experiences they had prior to the train episode were preparations for that day.

Coincidence you say? These individuals would never buy it. They believe Divine Providence was at work and will never accept otherwise.

There are countless stories like this one reported on a daily basis. Just watch the news or pick up a newspaper. So many of these so-called coincidences we will never know about, but I would bet they have been around since the beginning of time.

There are just too many things in life that happen at exactly the right time and place.

If you give credence to this then ask yourself, as I did, what kind of mastermind could orchestrate such happenings?

I call my mastermind God.

* * * * *

I tried, like so many of us, to lock away hurt and pain in my life, to forget these things even existed. I killed myself working tirelessly to forget. But in the end, trying to avoid pain caught up with me. I have learned that we need to *feel* the pain.

In her book *Radical Acceptance*, Tara Brach, PhD, presents a meaningful Sufi teaching that well attempts to explain so much of the anger, bitterness, and pain that we succumb to as humans. It states:

> "overcome any bitterness that
> may have come because you were

not up to the magnitude of pain
that was entrusted to you."

"Like the Mother of the
World, who carries the pain of
the world in her heart,

Each of us is part of her heart,

And therefore endowed with
a certain measure of cosmic pain."

"pain is an expression of
universal suffering (leading to)
radical acceptance."

This will lead us to our awakening and, eventually, to our healing.

Through my experiences, I have been made to
face my losses to recognize my soul as the center of
my being, and to find self-acceptance of who I am.
Finally, I have continued to make peace with myself.

My emotional breakdown, as terrible as it was,
served a very real purpose.

You can't put the
past behind you.
It has turned your flesh
into its own cupboard.
Not everything remembered
is useful, but it all
comes from the world to
be stored in you.
—Claudia Rankine,
Citizen: An American Lyric

Concluding Thoughts

I have had losses, but with each loss I have gained something in return. Through my daughter's illness and her father's death, I learned to handle extremely trying situations. I gained strength of character. I became more independent. Despite the sadness and grief, I continued to care for and protect my children, to trust myself more, and to rely on God's help. In the long run, I gained a new sense of compassion for others which lasts to this day.

In the loss of that early relationship, I gained a new perspective on judging character. I look to surround myself with strong, caring, honest individuals.

My losses and gains really were my children's as well, and in their own lives they, too, have survived losses and adversities. They have had to make difficult adjustments in their lives. But I have witnessed strength, drive, and perseverance in them. They demonstrate great compassion, forgiveness, and love. They are independent young professionals who live their convictions. I couldn't be prouder of them.

As long as we live, we will continue to experience the good and the not so good. It is a fact. It appears to be what we inherit as humans. But it is far more than that. I have come to believe it is a rite of passage between this world and the next.

We are born to grow, not just physically but mentally, emotionally, and intellectually as well. However, before we can do this, we need to encounter change. We need to endure opposition, pain, hardship, grief—and hopefully understanding, acceptance, and peace within at the end. For it is at birth that we receive the most wondrous of all gifts——the gift of a soul. It is this soul which has existed before our birth and will accompany us to the afterlife. And in between our soul will travel with us on the most amazing journey ever experienced——the journey of a lifetime.

I am not what I ought
to be,
I am not what I wish
to be,
I am not what I hope to be;
but, by the grace of God, I
am not what I was.
—John Newton

Sources

Berger, Susan, EdD, LICSW. *The Five Ways We Grieve: Finding Your Personal Path to Healing after the Loss of a Loved One*. Trumpeter, 2009.

Brach, Tara, PhD, *Radical Acceptance: Embracing Your Life with the Heart of a Buddha*. Bantam, 2003.

Moody, Raymond A., MD, *Life After Life*. Bantam, 1975.

Morse, Melvin, MD, and Perry, Paul. *Closer to the Light: Learning from Children's Near-Death Experiences*. Villard Books, 1990.

Morse, Melvin, MD, and Perry, Paul. *Transformed by the Light: The Powerful Effect of Near-Death Experiences on People's Lives*. Villard, 1992.

Taber, Gladys. *Another Path*. Lippincott, 1963.

White, Bob. *Bob White's Scrap Book*. Bob White Publishing, 1934.

Related Sources

Yahoo! www.jw.org/"the soul-spirit-meaning.
www.chabad.org
"What Is a Soul? What Is a Spirit?" www.biblecodeintro.com/intro9.html

encyclopedia.com/Encyclopedia of Science and Religion, Gale Group, Inc., 2003.

"Real Life Heroes of '15:17 to Paris.'" *The Pilot*, 9 Feb 2018, p. 22.

About the Author

Sue Berard-Goldberg resides in the Boston area with her family. She is a wife, mother, and grandmother. A speech pathologist for many years, Sue has presented workshops on language development, learning strategies, and writing processes, both in public school systems as well as in the private sector.

Sue has long been a supporter of animal welfare and rights. In 2013, she authored a children's book, *A Pumpkin for Thanksgiving*.